Conrad Kisch

Destination New York

Cornelsen

Cornelsen online http://www.cornelsen.de

1. Auflage, 1. Druck 2005

Druck: Narayana Press, Dänemark

ISBN 3-06-031224-9

Bestellnummer 312249

Fotos

Umschlag: Comstock

S. 1 o: Comstock, **S. 1 u:** Comstock, **S. 6/7:** Comstock, **S. 7:** Comstock, **S. 8/9:** Comstock, **S. 10 o:** Comstock, **S. 10 u:** Comstock, **S. 11:** Comstock, **S. 12:** Comstock, **S. 13:** Gyldendals Billedbibliotek, **S. 14:** The History of New York City, Portland House, **S. 15:** Gyldendals Billedbibliotek, **S. 16:** The History of New York City, Portland House, **S. 17:** The History of New York City, Portland House, **S. 18:** The History of New York City, Portland House, **S. 19:** Amerika, Samleren, **S. 20:** The American Nation, Longman, **S. 21 o:** The History of New York City, Portland House, **S. 21 u:** The History of New York City, Portland House, **S. 22:** The History of New York City, Portland House, **S. 23:** Comstock, **S. 24 o:** Comstock, **S. 24 u:** Reuters NewMedia Inc./Corbis, **S. 25:** Comstock, **S. 26 o:** Comstock, **S. 26 u:** Jacob Riis, **S. 27:** Comstock, **S. 28:** Bente Lindegaard/Polfoto, **S. 29:** Comstock, **S. 30:** Comstock, **S. 31:** Alan Schein Photography/Corbis, **S. 32:** Comstock, **S. 33:** Comstock, **S. 34:** Marc Asnin/Corbis, **S. 35:** Simon Høgsberg/Polfoto, **S. 36:** Jiri Rezac/Polfoto, **S. 36/37:** Michael Appleton/Corbis, **S. 38:** Nils Meilvang/Scanpix Danmark, **S. 38/39:** Graham Morrison/Scanpix Danmark, **S. 40:** Comstock, **S. 41:** Thomas Martin/Polfoto, **S. 42 o:** Digital Stock, **S. 42 u:** Comstock, **S. 43:** Comstock, **S. 44:** Kristin Wiborg, **S. 45:** Hubert Boesl/Polfoto, **S. 46:** Comstock, **S. 47:** Michael Boesen/Polfoto, **S. 48:** Comstock, **S. 49:** Comstock, **S. 50:** Mark Peterson/Corbis, **S. 51:** Julie Lemberger/Corbis, **S. 52:** Comstock, **S. 53:** Comstock, **S. 54:** Comstock, **S. 55:** Comstock, **S. 56:** Felix Ordonez/Reuters Newmedia Inc./Corbis, **S. 57:** Stone Les/Corbis Sygma, **S. 58:** Digital Stock, **S. 59:** Polfoto.

Contents

NEW JERSEY
MANHATTAN
BRONX
QUEENS
BROOKLYN
STATEN ISLAND
ATLANTIC OCEAN
Fair Lawn
BERGEN COMMUNITY COLLEGE
New Milford
Cresskill
Alpine
River Edge
Dumont
Bergenfield
Tenafly
PALISADES INTERSTATE PARK
SADDLE RIVER COUNTY PARK
Garden State Pkwy
Hackensack River
Palisades Interstate Pkwy
Elmwood Park
Rochelle Park
Maywood
Saddle Brook
Hackensack
Teaneck
Englewood
Garfield
Lodi
Bogota
Englewood Cliffs
Passaic
Passaic Expwy
Hasbrouck Heights
Ridgefield Park
OVERPECK COUNTY PARK
Leonia
Wallington
Wood Ridge
TETERBORO AIRPORT
Palisades Park
Fort Lee
G. Washington
FAIRLEIGH DICKINSON UNIV.
Ridgefield
Fairview
Cliffside Park
MEADOWLANDS SPORTS COMPLEX
Lyndhurst
Hackensack River
New Jersey Tpk
Tonnelle Av
John F. Kennedy Bl
NORTH HUDSON PARK
North Bergen
McCarter Hwy
North Arlington
Secaucus
West New York
Kearny
Union City
Lincoln Tunnel
STEVENS INST. OF TECH.
Hoboken
Holland Tunnel
LIBERTY STATE PARK
Ellis Island
STATUE OF LIBERTY
Governors Island
Newark Bay
Upper New York Bay
Bayonne
St. George
STATEN I. INST. OF ARTS AND SCIENCES
STATEN ISLAND FERRY TERMINAL
Port Richmond
STATEN ISLAND ZOO
SILVER LAKE PARK
Rosebank
Staten Island Expwy
Verrazano Nrws Br
FORT WADSWORTH
FORT HAMILTON
Hylan Bl
Hoffman Island
LIGHTHOUSE
New Dorp
Swinburne Island
Lower New York Bay
GREAT KILLS PARK
Hudson River
Henry Hudson Pkwy
RIVERDALE PARK
Washington Heights
TIBBETTS BROOK PARK
Bronxville
New Rochelle
IONA COLLEGE
Cross County Pkwy
Hutchinson Riv.
YONKERS RACEWAY
Bronx River Pkwy
Mount Vernon
Columbus Av
COLLEGE OF NEW ROCHELLE
Boston Post Rd
VAN CORTLANDT PARK
Broadway
Mosholu Pkwy
ST. PAUL'S CHURCH
Davids Island
GLEN ISLAND PARK
WOODLAWN CEMETERY
Jerome Park Res.
BRONX HIST. MUS.
Boston Post Rd
Hutchinson River Pkwy
BARTOW-PELL MANSION
Hart Island
Grand Concourse
FORDHAM UNIV.
NYC BOTANICAL GARDEN
Bronx Pelham Pkwy
PELHAM BAY PARK
BRONX ZOO
Cross Bronx Expwy
Bruckner Expw
City Island
BRONX MUS. FOR THE ARTS
Eastchester Bay
RIVERSIDE PARK
YANKEE STADIUM
Harlem River Dr
Harlem
Deegan Expw
Bruckner Expwy
SOUND VIEW PARK
Throgs Neck
COLUMBIA UNIV.
ST. ANN'S CHURCH
FERRY POINT PARK
Bronx Whitestone Br
FT. SCHUYLER
Throgs Neck Bridg
East River
Wards Island
Rikers Island
Whitestone
College Point
Little Neck Bay
CENTRAL PARK
LA GUARDIA AIRPORT
Francis Lewis Bl
Clearview Expwy
Cross Island Pkwy
Grand Central Pkwy
Astoria
F.D.R. Island
Long Island City
AMERICAN MUS. OF THE MOVING IMAGE
Astoria Bl
SHEA STADIUM
Flushing
Northern Bl
GRAND CENTRAL STATION
Queensboro Br
Northern Bl
FLUSHING MEADOWS CORONA PARK
Utopia Pkwy
KISSENA PARK
Queens Bl
QUEENS ZOO
14th St
Franklin D. Roosevelt Dr
Oakland St.
Brooklyn-Queens
Long Island Expwy
QUEENS COLLEGE C.U.N.Y.
CUNNINGHAM PARK
NYU
Houston St
Canal St
Maspeth
Woodhaven Bl
Queens Bl
ST. JOHN'S UNIV.
Union Tpk
Grand Central Pkwy
Hillside Av
West St
Williamsburg Br
Manhattan Br
Brooklyn Br
Williamsburg
BROOKLYN BOROUGH HALL GALLERY
BROOKLYN ACAD. OF MUSIC
Interborough Pkwy
FOREST PARK
Kew Gardens
Jamaica
Atlantic Av
Van Wyck Expwy
Bedford-Stuyvesant
HIGHLAND PARK
Ozone Park
Atlantic Av
AQUEDUCT RACETRACK
4th Av
MEMORIAL ARCH
BROOKLYN CHILDRENS MUS.
East New York
Conduit Av
ZOO
PROSPECT PARK
Prospect Expwy
Gowanus Expwy
Linden Bl
Nassau Expwy
Southern Pkwy
Flatbush Av
Kings Hwy
Shore Pkwy
JOHN F. KENNEDY INTERNATIONAL AIRPORT
Flatbush
Canarsie
CANARSIE BEACH PARK
BROOKLYN COLLEGE
Cross Bay Bl
Shore Pkwy
DYKER BEACH PARK
Canarsie Island
GATEWAY NATL. REC. AREA
BERGEN BEACH
Jamaica Bay
ROCKAWAY COMMUNITY PARK
Bensonhurst
Ocean Pkwy
Kings Hwy
MARINE PARK
FLOYD BENNET FIELD
Ruffle Bar
Gravesend
Shore Pkwy
Beach Channel Dr
KINGSBOROUGH COMMUNITY COLLEGE (CUNY)
Belle Harbor
Coney Island
Brighton Beach
JACOB RIIS PARK
Breezy Point

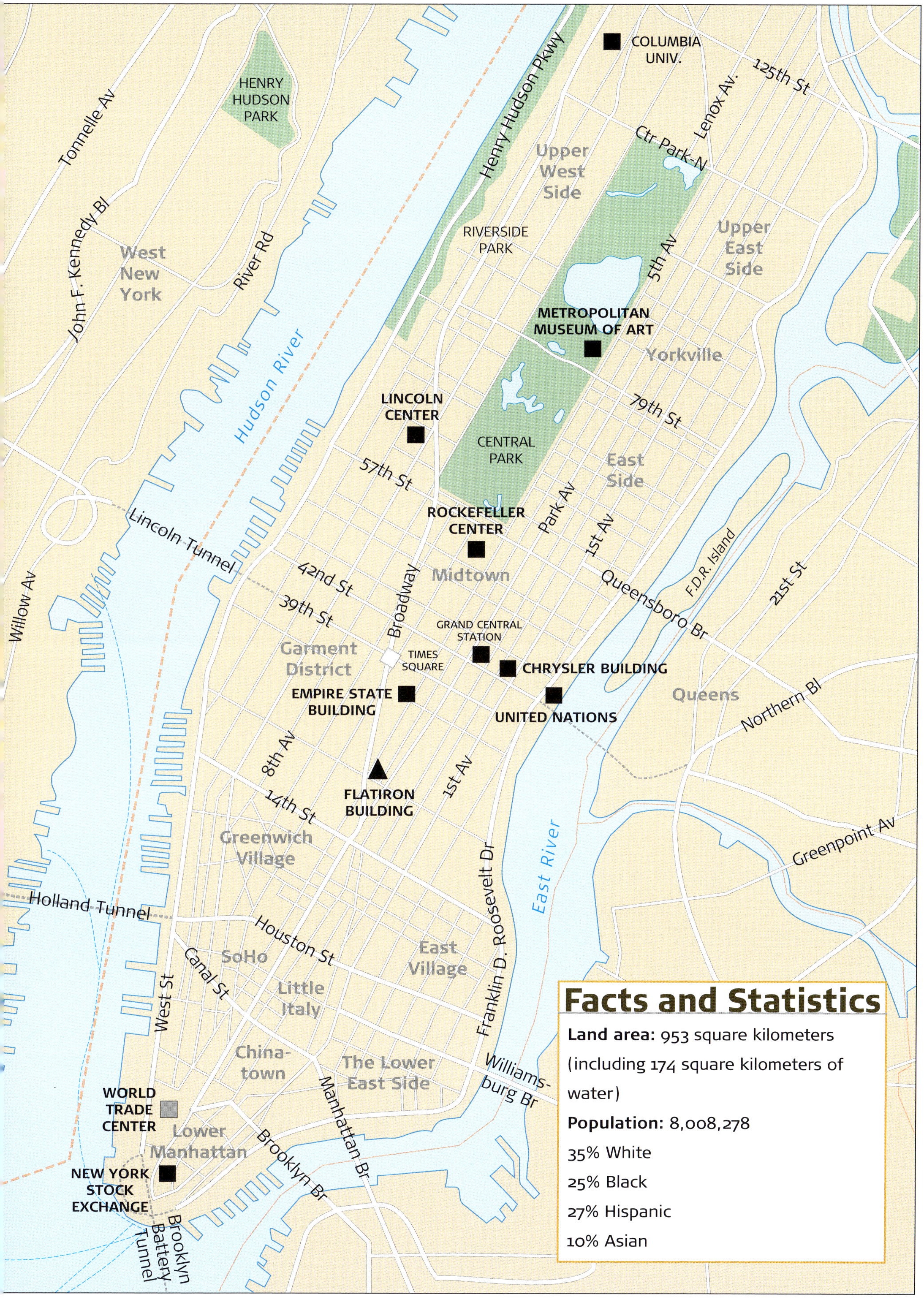

Facts and Statistics

Land area: 953 square kilometers (including 174 square kilometers of water)

Population: 8,008,278

35% White

25% Black

27% Hispanic

10% Asian

Welcome to the Big Apple!

New York City is the biggest city in the United States. More than eight million people live in New York City.

New York City is often called "the city that never sleeps"; something is always going on. Even the subway runs 24 hours a day.

Some of the richest people in the United States live in New York City. People sometimes pay up to a million dollars for a one-room apartment. But other New Yorkers live in slums where there are big problems with drugs and violence.

The Manhattan skyline.

New York City is not the capital of the United States; Washington is. New York City is not even the capital of New York State. But in some ways, New York City is the capital of the world. The headquarters of the United Nations is located in New York City, so diplomats and heads of states come to New York to discuss world problems.

New York City is the financial center of the United States and of the world. Choices made in offices in Wall Street affect millions of people, so New York City has become a symbol of the world influence of the United States. That is why some people hate New York City and its skyscrapers. They think America is a threat to their beliefs and lifestyles. On September 11, 2001, terrorists attacked the World Trade Center, New York's biggest skyscrapers, and thousands of people were killed. The lives of all New Yorkers changed forever.

New York City is the clothing capital of the United States, and 7th Avenue is called "Fashion Avenue." Many famous clothing designers like Calvin Klein, Ralph Lauren, and Donna Karan have their headquarters and factories in New York. Giant depart-

Times Square at night.

freaky facts:

Even New Yorkers don't know why New York City is called "the Big Apple." Some people think the name comes from a popular dance in the 1930's called "The Big Apple." Other people think it's from horse racing. If a horse won a race in New York City, it won a "Big Apple" as a reward.
The name really comes from a book written in 1909. In this book, the US is compared with a tree whose branches spread from one ocean to another and New York, "the Big Apple," is one of the fruits on that tree.

ment stores like Bloomingdale's, Macy's, Saks Fifth Avenue, and Lord and Taylor's are a paradise for shoppers. But poorly paid illegal immigrants make much of the clothing. Nearly three million New Yorkers were not born in the USA.

New York is the cultural capital of the United States. There are famous museums, ballet companies, libraries, universities, and jazz musicians. Broadway is well known for its theaters, but New York is also home to graffiti artists and hip-hop musicians.

New York City is called "the Big Apple." The city is as tempting as a big, red, delicious looking apple. Visitors want to take a big bite out of that apple and be part of New York.

New York City with the Statue of Liberty in the foreground.

freaky facts:

If you have seen the Batman movies, you have heard of Gotham City. Even before Batman, Gotham was a nickname for New York City. Gotham is really an old English word and means "goat town." In English folklore, Gotham is a town where all the people are fools!

Geography

New York, New York, it's a wonderful town
The Bronx is up and the Battery's down
The people ride in a hole in the ground
New York, New York, it's a wonderful town

– from Adolph Green and Leonard Bernstein's musical "On the Town."

New York is the name of a city, but it is also the name of one of the 50 states in the United States of America. New York City is located in the south-east corner of New York State. The city has one of the best natural harbors in the world. A big river, the Hudson, separates the city from the State of New Jersey. The Hudson River and New York's harbor were important for New York's development. New York became America's biggest port city and the place where millions of immigrants arrived from all around the world. Many of them stayed in New York.

The Staten Island Ferry.

freaky facts:

New York's biggest bargain is the Staten Island Ferry. The ferry sails between Manhattan and Staten Island, and the trip takes 25 minutes. Passengers get spectacular views of Manhattan's skyscrapers and the Statue of Liberty. In 1817, when the first steam ferry made the trip, it cost 25 cents for grown-ups and 12½ cents for children. From 1897 to 1972, the trip cost just 5 cents, but in 1972, the fare went up to 10 cents and to 25 cents in 1975. In 1990, it went up to 50 cents. How much does the ferry ride cost today? Since 1997, the ferry has been completely free for pedestrians and bicycles! Who says you can't get anything for free?

The Guggenheim Museum.

New York is so big that it has five sections or boroughs: Manhattan, the Bronx, Queens, Brooklyn, and Staten Island. These boroughs were once separate cities, towns, and villages. Only one borough, the Bronx, is on the mainland of the United States. The rest of New York City is on islands.

Manhattan is the most famous borough. When people think of New York City, they think of Manhattan. Manhattan is an island. It is surrounded by the Hudson River to the west, the Harlem River to the north, and the East River to the east. However, the East River is not really a river; it is really part of the Atlantic Ocean. The East River separates Long Island (with the boroughs of Brooklyn and Queens) from the rest of New York City.

Manhattan is where most tourists go. They visit the Empire State Building, theaters, museums, and department stores. They like to walk around neighborhoods like Chinatown, Greenwich Village, SoHo, and Harlem. Even though Manhattan is famous, it is actually the smallest borough. The island of Manhattan is about 21.7 kilometers long and only 3.8 kilometers wide at its widest point. About 1½ million people live in Manhattan.

Most New Yorkers don't live in Manhattan; they live in Brooklyn, Queens, and the Bronx. There are also big differences in population. Manhattan has a very mixed population. Half the people who live in Manhattan are white, about 15% are black, and 27% are Hispanic. The Bronx, on the other hand, has big slums and ghettos, so very few middle-class whites want to live there. About half the people who live in the Bronx are Hispanics, 31% are black, and just 14.5% are white. Then again, Staten Island is mainly white and middle-class.

Manhattan.

freaky facts:

11 million people live in the suburbs around New York City. This area is called The New York Metropolitan Area. It is defined as everything within 75 miles (120 kilometers) of Times Square. The New York Metropolitan Area includes parts of Pennsylvania, New Jersey, and Connecticut.

New York in winter.

New York City covers an area of about 953 square kilometers. That includes 174 square kilometers of water. London has about 7 million people, but it covers an area that is almost twice as big as New York. This means that New York City, and especially Manhattan, is much more crowded than London. There wasn't room to build outwards because of the water surrounding Manhattan, so New Yorkers had to build upwards. They built skyscrapers and big apartment buildings, while many Londoners live in small family houses. Geologically, New York City is old. In fact, some of New York City's bedrock is over 1.1 billion years old. Much of Manhattan consists of very hard stone like schist. This makes a good, solid, stabile foundation for building giant skyscrapers.

freaky facts:

New York City is as far south as Madrid and Rome. But New York City's climate is very different. New York is hot and humid in the summer. It can get as hot as 38° C. In the winter, however, the city gets a lot of snow and temperatures often fall to –5° C.

Nieuw Amsterdam

The first New Yorkers were American Indians. Village sites, pottery, heaps of shells, and Indian graves have been found in northern Manhattan. The Indians in the New York City area belonged to different tribes and clans and spoke different languages. Though the Indians have gone, many places in New York have Indian names. Manhattan is the best known Indian name. It probably means "island of hills," but no one today really knows.

In 1524, an Italian explorer named Giovanni da Verrazano became the first white man to see New York's harbor. But Verrazano didn't land. A storm blew up, and Verrazano's ship sailed away.

On the morning of September 11, 1609, a tiny Dutch ship called the *Halve Maen* or *Half Moon* with a crew of just twenty men moved past Staten Island and into New York's harbor. The captain's name was Henry Hudson. Hudson saw a long, narrow island, which the local Indians called Man-a-hat-ta.

Henry Hudson's first meeting with the Indians.

Nieuw Amsterdam in the 17th century.

West of the island was a great river. Hudson was looking for a way to get from Europe to the Far East. Unfortunately, America was in the way! Maybe this was a short cut? Hudson sailed up the river as far as he could. After a while, he realized that the river did not lead to China and Japan. But the Indians who lived along the river had something people wanted in Europe. They had beaver skins!

Henry Hudson was an Englishman, but sailed for the Dutch. Hudson claimed the land he had discovered for the Netherlands. He called the land *Nieuw Nederlandt* – the New Netherlands. Today the river he discovered is called the Hudson River.

The first permanent settlers came to Manhattan in 1624. These Dutch settlers built a town and fort on the southern tip of Manhattan. They called their city *Nieuw Amsterdam*, or New Amsterdam. In 1626, the Dutch bought Manhattan from the Indians for just $24.

freaky facts:

In 1610, Hudson sailed back to America. Hudson was still looking for a short cut to the Far East. In Canada, Hudson found a huge body of water, which is now called Hudson Bay. Hudson thought the bay must be the way to the Pacific Ocean. But it wasn't. Hudson and his crew stayed in Hudson Bay for the winter. The men froze and starved. Finally, they mutinied and put Hudson and his son in an open boat. They were never seen again.

freaky facts:

American history books always write that the Dutch paid the Indians 60 guilders or $24. Of course, $24 was a lot more money in 1626 than it is today, but it was still a bargain. However, the Indians did not have the same idea of private property that Europeans have. They probably did not know they were "selling" their land.

By the 1650s, a thousand people lived in Nieuw Amsterdam. Old drawings show us that the town looked like a tiny version of Dutch cities like Amsterdam. There were narrow brick houses with stepped gables, a canal, and windmills. To protect Nieuw Amsterdam from the Indians, the Dutch built a wall along the northern edge of the town. Today, Wall Street marks the spot. However, land is so expensive in Manhattan that there are very few old buildings left and none from the time of the Dutch. But if we go to Brooklyn, we can find the oldest house in New York State, the Pieter Claesen Wyckoff house, a simple farmhouse built in 1642.

Nieuw Amsterdam drew settlers from many countries. 18 languages were spoken. The Bronx was even named after a Dane, Jonas Bronck, who was the first European to live there. Many of the people who came to Nieuw Amsterdam came for religious freedom. There were French Protestants. There were Jews. There were even English-speaking Protestants called Quakers who had to escape from the nearby English colonies in New England. In fact, the second oldest house in New York City, the Bowne House from 1661, belonged to an English Quaker. Today, the house is a national monument to religious freedom. But there were people who

freaky facts:

Theodore ("Teddy") Roosevelt was the only US president born in New York City. Roosevelt was president from 1900 to 1908. Roosevelt was a famous hunter, but he also tried to protect wildlife, so the Teddy bear was named after him.

Theodore "Teddy" Roosevelt.

did not come to Manhattan freely. The Dutch brought the first African slaves to Nieuw Amsterdam in 1626. There were slaves in New York until 1827.

On August 29, 1664, disaster hit Nieuw Amsterdam. The English decided to take over the Dutch colony and sent 4 warships and 450 soldiers. The Dutch gave up without a fight. Nieuw Amsterdam became New York. In 1673, the Dutch retook Manhattan – this time the English gave up without fighting. One year later, the Dutch soldiers left Manhattan forever. The Dutch had traded Manhattan for Surinam in South America. They thought that sugar from Surinam was worth more than New York City!

The Dutch did leave some things behind – freedom of religion and the people's right to elect their own city government. Two of America's most famous presidents, Theodore Roosevelt and his cousin Franklin D. Roosevelt, were descendants of early Dutch settlers. Though New Yorkers no longer speak Dutch, they did keep a few Dutch words. The Dutch word for a little cake is *koekje*. This has become the American word "cookie." And of course, everyone has heard of Santa Claus. His original Dutch name is *Sinter Klaas*.

New York City still has many Dutch place names. Harlem, for example, is named after the city of *Haarlem* in Holland. New York City's flag is blue, white, and orange – the colors of the 17th century Dutch flag. The city's coat of arms shows a windmill, a Dutchman, an Indian, two beavers, and two barrels of flour. They reflect the origins of the huge city of today.

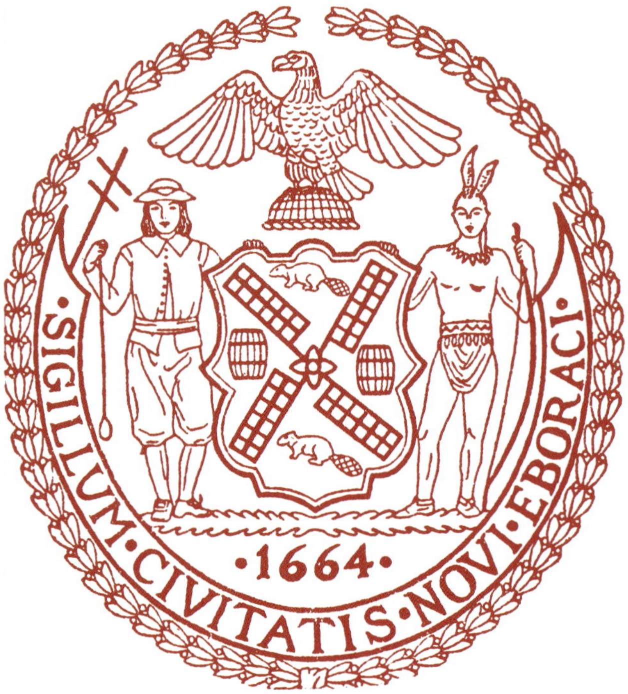

New York City's coat of arms.

English New York

Lord Cornbury dressed as a woman.

The English settlers tried to turn their town into a place that would remind them of their old homes in England. Street names like Hanover Square, Maiden Lane, and Thames Street were copied from London. Manhattan's oldest church, St. Paul's Chapel on Broadway, looks just like St. Martin's-in-the-Fields on Trafalgar Square in London.

New York City grew. By 1775, there were some 20,000 New Yorkers – including thousands of slaves. Some of these New Yorkers were a bit strange. Lord Cornbury was governor of New York between 1702 and 1708. His Lordship looked so much like his cousin, Queen Anne, that he liked to dress up like a woman and walk around town. Lady Cornbury, the governor's wife, liked to steal things when she visited people's homes. In the end, Lord Cornbury owed so much money that he was put in jail and sent back to England.

Another New Yorker was Captain William Kidd. Kidd was born in Scotland in 1645 and came to New York in 1691. At home, William Kidd was a respected merchant, businessman, and gentleman. Kidd gave money to the church and the poor. In those days, England was always at war with France. Kidd was hired by the king to capture French ships and pirate ships. Instead, Kidd became a pirate himself. He was caught and hanged at Execution Dock in London on May 23, 1701. Many people think that Kidd's treasure was buried on Gardiner's Island just off the coast of Long Island. A lot of people have looked, but so far, no one has found the treasure. Maybe you will be the lucky one!

Captain Kidd.

Violence has always been part of New York's history. New York's black slaves were badly treated. In 1712, 23 slaves planned to revolt and kill all the white people in New York. The revolt was brutally put down. Afterwards, at least 21 blacks were executed. Some were slowly burned alive or tortured by having their arms and legs broken. In 1741, there was fear that the slaves would revolt again. This time, 154 blacks were put in jail, 14 were burned alive, 18 were hanged, 71 were sent to the West Indies, and even four whites were executed for helping the black slaves. One of the whites was accused of planning to become king of New York if the black rebellion succeeded.

New York and the American Revolution

In 1766, New York paid £1,000 for a statue of King George III. The statue arrived in 1770 and was placed in a little park at Bowling Green and surrounded by a fence. The fence is still there. The statue isn't. It was pulled down just 6 years later. What happened?

During the 18th century, Great Britain fought many wars and owed a great deal of money. Britain wanted the American colonies to pay some of the costs. The Americans felt it was unfair of the British to tax them. Furthermore, Americans did not like the fact that Great Britain would only let American ships sail to Britain and buy British goods. Americans wanted to do business with anybody they liked.

In 1773, Americans threw a cargo of tea into Boston harbor. They were protesting against a British tax on tea. On April 22, 1774, New Yorkers threw tea into the Hudson River. The British government got angry and decided to punish the colonies. Soon Americans and British soldiers were fighting each other. The American Revolution had begun. George Washington was chosen to lead an American army against the British, and on July 4, 1776, the United States of America declared its independence. New Yorkers celebrated by tearing down the statue of King George.

King George III.

Americans throwing tea into Boston harbor.

Their celebration did not last long. The Americans had chased the British from Boston. Now the British navy and army sailed to New York. By the end of September, the British had captured all of Manhattan and made New York City their headquarters. They would be there for the rest of the war. Four days after the British took over, one fourth of the city burned down. Even so, many people who were loyal to the king came to the city for protection. Other people came because they thought they could make money by selling things to the British and business boomed.

In the end, the British lost the war. On November 25, 1783, the British left New York City forever, and those loyal to the king had to leave, too. From now on, New York would be an American city. On December 4th, Washington said farewell to his officers in Fraunces Tavern at the corner of Pearl and Broad streets. Today, visitors can eat at the tavern or visit its museum.

freaky facts:

The American Revolution was very much a civil war. Many New York families were split. The Clinton family numbered George Clinton, a British royal governor, and his son Sir Henry Clinton, a British general.

Sir Henry's nephews, George and James, became American generals during the Revolution and even fought against their uncle in a battle. Later, George became the first governor of New York following independence. De Witt Clinton, James's son, also became New York's governor.

New York Grows

On April 30, 1789, George Washington was sworn in as president of the United States in New York's city hall. New York had become the nation's capital. Sadly, it was soon moved to Philadelphia and then to Washington, D.C. On April 30, 1790, George Washington left the city, never to return. However, in 1792 a group of 24 men started the New York Stock Exchange. The stock exchange helped raise money to invest in shipping, canals, and industries. Today it is the most important financial market in the world.

Since America was independent, American ships could sail anywhere they wanted to, and New York's international position grew stronger. Ships from New York sailed to China and brought back tea and porcelain. New York's role as gateway to America

George Washington at New York's City Hall, April 30, 1789.

New York's harbor around 1830.

became even more important after the first successful steamship in the world, the Clermont, started sailing on the Hudson in 1807. Now, passengers and cargo didn't have to wait for a good wind. They could sail whenever they wanted. In 1825, the Erie Canal opened. The canal connected the Hudson with the Great Lakes, and the cost of moving one ton of cargo from New York City to Buffalo dropped from $120 to just $6. Because of the canal, New York became America's main port and half of all imports to America passed through the city.

New York grew. In 1790, there were 33,131 New Yorkers. Ten years later, there were 60,489 people in the city. By 1810, 96,373 people lived in New York. And more and more people were pouring in!

A commission was formed to plan the city's growth. In 1811, the plan was ready. Because the chief engineer was named John Randall, Jr., it was called the Randall plan. The Randall plan laid out Manhattan's famous grid of north-south avenues crossed by east-west streets. This grid stretched from East Houston Street to 155th Street. Everything that got in the way of the grid was removed. Farms, fields, houses, hills, rivers, and woods were leveled. Of course, people laughed back in 1811. They said it would take hundreds of years before people would move to Harlem. 155th Street was more than 11 kilometers away from the city! Remember, back in 1811 there were no trains, cars, or buses to move big numbers of people. The Randall plan is an amazing example of planning for the future. By 1898, nearly three and a half million people lived in New York. New York City had become the second biggest city in the world. Only London was bigger.

The Randall Plan.

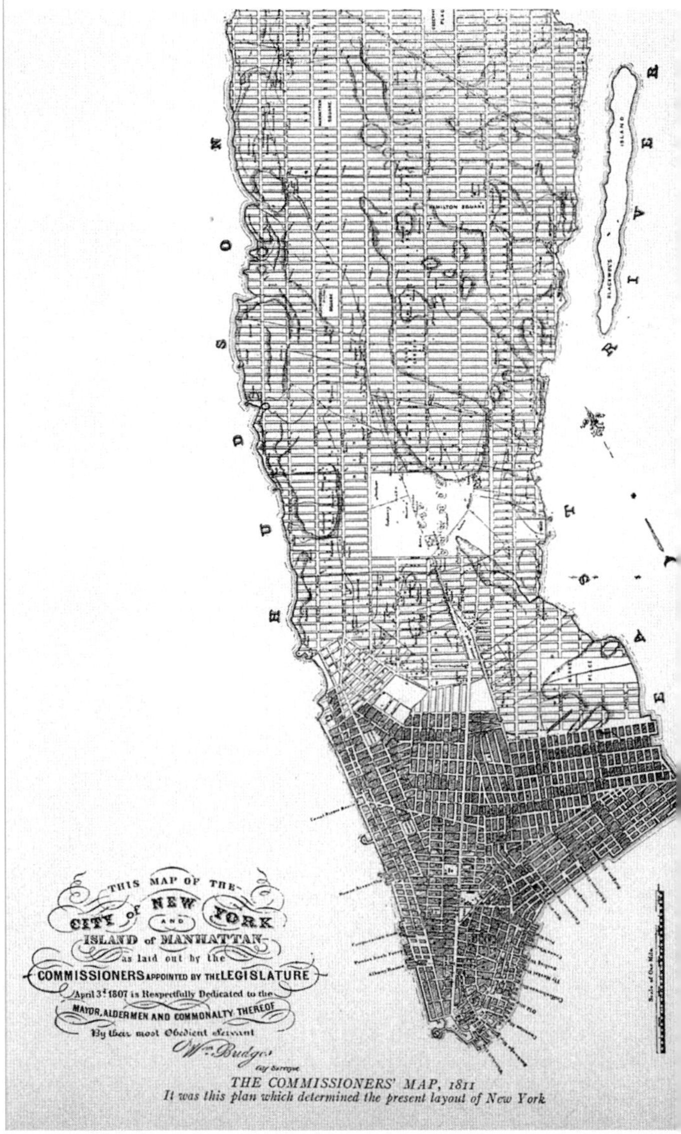

Central Park

The city planners who designed the system of east-west streets and north-south avenues forgot one important thing. They forgot that people need fresh air and green trees. The 1811 plan did include some small green spaces. Most of them were never built. Something had to be done. In 1856, the city spent 5.5 million dollars to buy land for a big park. The park stretches from 59th Street to 110th Street and from 5th Avenue to 8th Avenue. It covers an area of 377 hectares.

At the time, many people thought the city was crazy. New York City only reached as far north as 34th Street. That was about 2 kilometers away. Who would ever use the park? However, in 1884 the first luxury apartment building opened on 72nd

freaky facts:

Central Park may look natural, but it isn't. It took 4,000 men 13 years to make the park. They had to drain swamps, dig lakes, and plant 500,000 trees and bushes.

freaky facts:

The Dakota building is pretty spooky-looking. It was even used in the horror movie Rosemary's Baby. Many famous movie stars have lived there as well as John Lennon from the Beatles. John Lennon was murdered in front of the building. In memory of John Lennon, a part of Central Park just outside the building is now called Strawberry Fields. Strawberry Fields was one of Lennon's most famous songs.

Street and Central Park West. People made fun of the building. They called it The Dakota. They said it was just about as far away as the state of Dakota in the Wild West. But the architect decided he liked the name. He even decorated the front door with a sculpture of an Indian with arrows.

Today Central Park is right in the middle of the busiest part of Manhattan and is surrounded by tall apartment buildings, skyscrapers, and luxury hotels. The park is every New Yorker's backyard. It's where children go to sail toy boats, roller-skate in the summer, ice-skate in the winter, and play baseball. They climb around on statues of the characters from the children's book *Alice in Wonderland*. They can hear stories read out loud at the statue of Hans Christian Andersen. They can ride on an old-fashioned carrousel. Grown-ups come to rent a rowboat, go for a walk, listen to concerts, see plays, and just relax. The park even has an excellent zoo.

Statue of the characters in Alice in Wonderland.

Ellis Island with the Statue of Liberty in the background.

New Yorkers and their Neighborhoods

What is a typical New Yorker like? That question is hard to answer. Since New York City is always changing, the people who live there change too.

To start off with, New York was a Dutch town. Then it became an English city. During the first half of the 19th century, so many Irishmen came that New York was virtually an Irish city. Later on, however, Italians and Jews formed the largest ethnic groups in the city. Then many blacks started to arrive. Today the city can be said to be white, Hispanic, and black, but right now, many Asians are moving to New York. Each of these waves of immigrants has changed and shaped the city.

Why did these immigrants come to New York? For many people around the world, the US was – and still is – the land of opportunity. People come to America to get away from bad conditions in their home countries. They come to find work and to make better lives for themselves and their children. Though blacks have lived in New York since the 17th century, many of the city's blacks are immigrants, too. Black families came from America's southern states to escape poverty. Today many blacks come from Jamaica, Haiti, and Africa.

freaky facts:

The Statue of Liberty in New York's harbor became a symbol of America for millions of immigrants. It is also a symbol of New York City. The statue, built in 1886, was a gift from France to the people of the United States. That is why there is a little version of the Statue of Liberty in Paris. The statue was designed by Frederic Auguste Bartholdi. Gustave Eiffel, the man who built the Eiffel Tower in Paris, built the framework that supports the statue. The statue is 46.05 meters tall. It weighs 204 tons and stands on a 47-meter tall pedestal.

Around 23½ million people came to the US from 1880 to 1920. Since New York City was America's biggest port, most immigrants arrived here. Between 1892 and 1954, immigrants were received on an island in New York's harbor. This island, Ellis Island, became known as the "Island of Hope" and the "Island of Tears." Hope for the 98% of the immigrants who were allowed to come into the US. Tears for the 2% who were sent back. People were sent back if they couldn't take care of themselves, were criminals, mentally ill, or had health problems like heart disease or eye diseases. Immigrants were asked questions like: What is your name? How much money do you have? Do you have a job waiting for you? The last question was tricky. If they answered yes, they would be sent back. A law passed in 1882 made it against the law for anyone to be hired before coming to the USA.

All together, around 16 million immigrants passed through Ellis Island. Sometimes there were as many as 11,000 in one day. About 100 million Americans are descended from the immigrants who arrived at Ellis Island. That is nearly half of all the people in the US.

An immigrant in his home. Photo by Jacob Riis.

Many of the immigrants stayed in New York City. There were German, Jewish, Italian, Irish, Polish, Russian, Greek, Hungarian, and Scandinavian neighborhoods – and many others, too. These neighborhoods had stores, restaurants, cafés, and theaters where the immigrants could feel at home. New York had, and still has, newspapers written in dozens of languages. In Brooklyn, there is even a Norwegian newspaper, *Nordisk Tidende*. Some of these neighborhoods were dreadful slums. The immigrants often lived under terrible conditions. A Danish-born journalist, Jacob Riis, took photos of the slums and wrote a book called *How the Other Half Lives* (1890). The book shocked many Americans.

Gradually, the immigrants or their children got better jobs. They became part of American society. They left the slum neighborhoods and moved to better areas, and new waves of immigrants moved in. This process is still going on. Puerto Ricans now live in what used to be the Jewish Lower East Side.

Most New Yorkers are proud of their ethnic origins, and they celebrate them in big parades on 5th Avenue like the Saint Patrick's Day Parade for the Irish. Saint Patrick converted the Irish to Christianity and is the patron saint of Ireland. On Saint Patrick's Day people wear green, paint themselves green, and even drink green beer.

However, many of New York's ethnic neighborhoods are dying out. Tourists go to Little Italy to eat at Italian restaurants, sit at cafés, and buy Italian groceries. At one time, 40,000 Italians lived there. But now, there are only about 5,000 Italians left. The apartments above the stores are either empty or Chinese immigrants live there.

Little Italy.

Harlem.

Facts and Statistics

New York's Foreign-Born Population in 2000: 2,871,032

Latin American: 1,511,419

Asian: 686,599

European: 557,492

African: 92,435

North American: 18,066

Oceanian: 4,982

Other ethnic neighborhoods are thriving. Large parts of the city are Spanish-speaking. There is also a little India, a little Korea, and a Russian-Jewish neighborhood called little Odessa. In Borough Park, Williamsburg, and Crown Heights in Brooklyn, you can find religious Jews who wear long black coats and old-fashioned broad, black hats. Many of them work as jewelers and diamond cutters in New York's diamond district on 47th Street.

One famous ethnic area is Harlem. Harlem has long been a cultural center for America's blacks. "The Harlem Renaissance" was a literary movement in the 1920s. It showed all Americans, also whites, that there were talented black authors.

Not all of Harlem is poor. Middle-class blacks and black artists and intellectuals live in areas like "Striver's Row" and "Sugar Hill." One Harlem resident was Thurgood Marshall who became a Supreme Court judge. Other famous blacks who lived in Harlem were jazz musicians like Cab Calloway, Count Basie, and Duke Ellington.

freaky facts:

Not all of Harlem is black. East Harlem, or El Barrio ("the neighborhood"), is mostly Puerto Rican.
In fact, it is the biggest Spanish-speaking area in New York City.

China Town.

In the 1960s and 1970s, Harlem had a lot of problems with drugs and crime. Today Harlem is getting safer. Even whites are starting to move in. Tourists come to taste "soul food" – traditional black cooking from down south – and hear jazz, blues, soul, and gospel music.

Chinatown is the city's most crowded and exotic neighborhood. It is the biggest Chinese community in the USA. Between 70,000 and 150,000 people live there. No one is quite sure! For many immigrants from China, this is their first stop. They get a job in one of the many Chinese restaurants or sew clothing in the Garment District. 10 or 15 people may share a tiny apartment, so they can save up money. After a few years, they may try to open a restaurant of their own and hire new immigrants to work as waiters and cooks.

The number of New Yorkers born outside of the USA is going up. In 1990, 28.4% of New Yorkers were born outside of the USA. In 2000, the figure had gone up to 35.9%.

Though New York has lots of ethnic neighborhoods, most neighborhoods are ethnically mixed. All of them, however, have a special character. There are wealthy neighborhoods like the Upper East Side and the more middle-class Upper West Side. There is also Greenwich Village. The Village, as New Yorkers call it, has always been different. Even the streets are different; they don't run east to west like the rest of Manhattan. The Village used to be the place where actors, artists, and musicians lived. In the 60s and 70s, it was the place for hippies. These days, it is too expensive for artists. So artists started moving to empty factories and warehouses in SoHo. Now SoHo is getting expensive, so artists and galleries are moving to other neighborhoods.

SoHo.

freaky facts:

SoHo has nothing to do with Soho in London. It is short for "South of Houston Street."

Some neighborhoods are not places where people live. They are places where people work or shop. The Garment District is the center of New York's clothing industry. Midtown Manhattan consists mostly of office buildings and stores. It is also famous for Rockefeller Center. Rockefeller Center has giant office buildings. But it also has elegant stores and a big plaza. The plaza is an outdoor restaurant in summer and an ice skating rink in winter. Rockefeller Center also has Radio City Music Hall. With 5,900 seats it is the biggest indoor theater in the world.

Lower Manhattan, where New York City started, is now the Financial District. Here are giant office buildings, too. The Financial District used to be completely deserted in the weekends. In recent years, however, people have moved into new apartment buildings. This has brought new life to New York's oldest streets.

Rich and Poor

New York City has always been a place where people come to make money – and to spend it. As far back as the 19th century, you could read in books, "Strangers coming to New York are struck with the fact that there are but two classes in the city – the poor and the rich."

This is still true today. Relatively few middle-class families live in Manhattan. Housing is just too expensive. Everything else is expensive, too. Food costs more in the city because the grocery stores have to pay high rents. Even taxes are higher. Middle-class families live in Staten Island, Queens, or have left the city completely. If you want a nice big house, green grass, and good schools, you have to move to the suburbs. Even many of the suburbs are expensive. People move further and further away from New York to be able to afford a house. Many people who work in the city drive two hours to get to work and to get home again.

Suburban houses.

The Plaza.

New York is the banking and investment center of the United States. This means that a lot of very wealthy people have always lived in the city. A hundred years ago, some of the richest people in the United States – and in the world – built their houses on 5th Avenue. That way they had views of Central Park. 5th Avenue became known as "Millionaires' Mile." These houses looked like royal palaces or castles. Today, even millionaires cannot afford to live like that in New York. Most of the old mansions have been torn down and replaced by luxury apartment buildings. But some of them have been turned into museums. There are so many of these museums that 5th Avenue is now called "Museum Mile." Henry Clay Frick, one of the owners of U.S. Steel turned his house into a museum in 1919. The Frick Museum is furnished with Frick's original furniture and valuable paintings. The museum gives visitors a good idea of how the rich used to live.

How expensive is Manhattan? New York's best neighborhood, the Upper East Side, is called the "Gold Coast." You need a lot of money to live there. A studio or one-bedroom apartment can cost up to a million dollars. A three-bedroom apartment costs between 3 and 4 million dollars. Of course, those are just the cheap ones. A good "family apartment" with a nice view of Central Park might cost up to 20 million dollars. Some of these apartments have private rooftop gardens. If you want to buy a townhouse, count on spending between 8 and 25 million dollars. You could also rent a "family apartment." That could cost you up to $11,000 per month. On top of that, you will probably want to send your children to exclusive private schools. That can cost you another $2,000 each month. On nearby 5th Avenue you can go shopping at famous jewelry stores like Cartier and Tiffany, expensive department stores like Bergdorf Goodman and Saks 5th

Avenue, or have afternoon tea at the Plaza Hotel. On Madison Avenue you can browse for European antiques, buy English perfumes, or handmade shirts. Perhaps you would like to buy a pair of $500 shoes? For dinner, you might pay a couple of hundred dollars at a good restaurant.

On the other hand, there are many slums and poor neighborhoods in New York. Over 20% of all New Yorkers are officially poor. Poor people came to the city to look for jobs. Unfortunately, many industries left the city. There wasn't need for people without skills or a good education. This meant that they became unemployed. Poor people are dependent on welfare payments from the city or receive food stamps. Food stamps are special stamps people can use in grocery stores instead of cash. They cannot buy cigarettes or beer with them.

Poor neighborhoods have a lot more crime. Often crime is connected to drugs. People take drugs to forget how bad or hopeless their lives are. Then they have to steal to get enough money to buy the drugs. Young people are tempted to sell drugs because it is a fast way to make a lot of money. Drugs lead to gang violence, murders, and more crime.

Park Avenue.

freaky facts:

There is one problem all New Yorkers share. It doesn't matter if they are rich or poor. Cockroaches! Cockroaches can be found in all neighborhoods in the city. They are in apartments, restaurants, and hotels. You can even find them on the top floors of skyscrapers. Cockroaches can spread diseases, so New Yorkers use a lot of time and money trying to get rid of these pests.

Poor neighborhoods can be quite close to rich ones. If you look at a map of Manhattan, you can find a street called Park Avenue. Park Avenue is very wide because it is built over railroad tracks. There are many blocks of luxury apartment buildings; and Park Avenue is probably the wealthiest area in the whole USA.

If we continue northwards on Park Avenue, you will discover that the railroad tracks come up from below ground at East 99th Street. The neighborhood suddenly changes. Rich people don't want to live near noisy railroad tracks. You are now in a slum. The statistics tell their tale. Below 99th Street, 899 people received welfare benefits in 2002, and there were 79 reports of child abuse. North of 99th Street, 15,303 persons were on welfare, and there were 794 cases of child abuse.

Children playing in the South Bronx.

Homeless man.

Today, the price of housing is so high that middle-class people cannot live in areas like the "Gold Coast." Instead, they move into Manhattan's poor neighborhoods and convert the buildings. This is called "gentrification." The poor people get pushed out. Since they have to live somewhere, they leave Manhattan and move to New York City's other boroughs. So while the average income is going up in Manhattan, it is actually going down in Queens and other parts of the city. The Bronx, for example, used to be a largely middle-class area. Today the middle class has left, and the Bronx has some of the toughest neighborhoods in the city. While the average income in Manhattan is $43,000 a year, in the Bronx, it is only $14,000.

Much of Harlem used to be a dangerous slum. Nowadays, a building boom is going on. People are moving into luxury condominiums and co-ops. Harlem is now attracting whites, middle-class blacks, Asians, and Europeans. There are families with children and gay couples. In Harlem you can still buy a one-bedroom apartment for $100,000 to $300,000 and a townhouse for just 1.2 million dollars. That may sound like a lot of money to you, but compared to other parts of Manhattan, that is cheap.

New York's poorest people don't even live in slums or ghettoes. They are the homeless. They live in the streets. They live under bridges and in tunnels. Some of them make their homes in the subways. Others turn to special shelters for the homeless. No one knows how many homeless people there are in New York. Around 37,000 people use the shelters every night. Perhaps 10% of the homeless are people who are mentally ill. Some of them are drug addicts. But many of the homeless are just people who have had a tough break and lost their jobs.

New York's Finest

Big cities have big problems. New York City, like most really big cities, has a lot of crime. Many people think New York is a very dangerous city – maybe because they have seen so many crime movies and TV programs that take place in New York. Even many New Yorkers are afraid.

Crime and violence have always been problems in the city. In the 19th century, gangs of poor Irish immigrants had bloody battles with gangs of native New Yorkers. Some of these gangs had up to 1,200 members!

The worst riots in the city's history took place in 1863, during America's Civil War. The U.S. Army needed soldiers to fight the southern Confederate states. There weren't enough volunteers, so the government started to draft men into the army. Between 50,000 and 70,000 New Yorkers went crazy. As many as 2,000 people were killed and 8,000 were wounded. In the end, 10,000 soldiers had to be called in to stop the riots.

Even the police sometimes rioted! Originally, New York had no daytime police, just night watchmen. New York City finally got a uniformed police force in 1853, called the Municipal Police. In 1857, the State of New York set up their own police force for the city. They called their police force the Metropolitan Police and ordered the city to get rid of the Municipal Police. The two police forces fought each other. The Metropolitan Police tried to capture City Hall and arrest the mayor. In the meantime, criminals and gangs ran wild. They murdered, robbed, and battled each other, too. In the end, the army had to stop everyone – the criminals and the police.

Actually, New York City is a lot safer today than it has been for a long time. In 2002, there were 82 murders in Manhattan. That is the lowest number since the year 1900! As late as 1990, there were 503 murders in Manhattan. Today, New York City has one of the lowest crime rates in the USA. The USA has 182 cities with more than 100,000 people. New York comes in at 136 when it comes to crime.

freaky facts:

Policemen are not allowed to cross the border from one state to another. New York City is in New York State. But the city is connected by bridges, tunnels, and trains to the state of New Jersey where many of the city's workers live. These are some of the busiest roads and railroads in the whole country. What happens if someone commits a crime in New York City and drives to New Jersey? Well, there is a special police force called the Port Authority Police. These 1,400 policemen and policewomen are allowed to operate in New York and New Jersey within a radius of 25 miles (40 kilometers) of the Statue of Liberty. They take care of traffic control, crime prevention, rescue operations, emergencies, and even fire fighting.

How come New York is so good at fighting crime? For one thing, the city has a "Zero Tolerance Policy." They stop people who drink alcohol in the street, urinate in public, beg, play loud radios, or write graffiti. By cracking down on these minor problems, the police send the message that serious crimes will not be put up with. Normal New Yorkers feel safer and say that the quality of life in the city has improved. The police are also trying to rid the streets of illegal drugs and guns. As part of "Operation Cash for Guns," people were given $100 for every gun they handed in. The police received more than 1,700 weapons.

A drug bust in Harlem.

A New York City fire engine.

Though crime has gone down in New York City, it has not vanished. There were 32,310 burglaries, 26,783 robberies, 28,647 auto thefts, and 1,288 cases of rape in 2002. Parts of New York like the South Bronx and Bedford-Stuyvesant in Brooklyn really are dangerous. However, if you simply avoid buying or selling drugs, your chances of becoming a victim are not very big.

To keep the city safe, there are 39,110 police officers in the N.Y.P.D. – the New York Police Department. These officers are known as "New York's Finest." Being a police officer is a tough job. Many officers have lost their lives in the line of duty. Americans regard these men and women as real heroes, and police series on TV are a popular form of entertainment.

The officers of the N.Y.P.D. are not New York's only heroes. A big city has a lot of fires. In 2002, there were over 50,000 fires. The New York Fire Department's ambulances also went out to more than 150,000 medical emergencies. Firefighters have dangerous jobs, too. Television viewers around the world saw the brave men of the New York Fire Department try to save people when the World Trade Center was attacked on September 11, 2001. 343 firefighters were caught inside the buildings and killed when the towers collapsed. Along with the firefighters, 23 New York City policemen and 37 police officers from the Port Authority Police died on September 11th.

freaky facts:

Terrorism is not new. During the American Civil War, 8 secret agents from the South tried to burn down New York City. They set fire to 19 hotels, two theaters, a museum, several ships, stores, factories, and lumberyards. Fortunately, all the fires were quickly put out. The secret agents escaped to Canada. Only one of them was ever caught and hanged.

A firefighter in the ruins of the World Trade Center.

Skyscrapers

The Manhattan skyline.

When people think of New York City, they think of skyscrapers. To build skyscrapers you need two things. You have to have elevators – no one wants to walk up twenty, thirty or a hundred floors. And you have to have cheap, strong steel.

Traditional buildings are kept upright by their walls. Brick or stone walls support roofs and floors. The bigger the building, the thicker the walls have to be. If a building is much taller than 6 floors, the walls get so thick that they take up valuable space. In skyscrapers, a steel frame holds up the roof and floors. This frame works much the same way your skeleton supports your body.

freaky facts:

The first skyscraper in America, the 10-story Home Insurance Building, was not built in New York. It was built in Chicago in 1885. To start off with, Chicago was the leader when it came to building skyscrapers!

The early skyscrapers often had heavy-looking stone walls. People were nervous about these giant new buildings, so the architects made the walls look nice and solid so people wouldn't be scared. In reality, the walls only supported their own weight and didn't support the buildings. Today, most skyscrapers are just covered with thin walls of metal and glass.

Progress was fast. In 1902, the world's tallest skyscraper was New York's 86-meter high, 21-story tall Flatiron Building. The building has a funny triangular shape. It looks just like an old-fashioned iron for ironing clothes.

By the late 1920s architects and builders were competing to see who could build the tallest building. They kept their plans secret, so rival builders wouldn't know how big their new skyscrapers were going to be. One of New York's most famous skyscrapers is the Chrysler Building, built for a car company. The building was supposed to be 282 meters high. Then the architect, William van Alen, heard that his former partner, H. Craig Severance, was building a skyscraper for the Bank of Manhattan. Severance was going to put a flagpole on top of his building. That would make the bank's building 61 centimeters taller than the Chrysler Building! Mr. Chrysler wanted his building to be the tallest. They formed a secret plan and built a giant spire inside the top floors of the building. Then they waited until the Bank of Manhattan Building was nearly finished. When it was too late for the Bank of Manhattan Building to catch up, they got ready. They raised up the spire. Then they attached it to the top of the building in just 90 minutes. Now the Chrysler Building was 319 meters tall! Unfortunately for Mr. Chrysler, it was the world's tallest building for just one year.

The Flatiron Building.

freaky facts:

Many skyscrapers were built by Mohawk Indians. Mohawks get used to high places because they walk along cliffs in their homelands in the border area between New York State and Canada.

The Chrysler Building.

The Chrysler Building is probably New York's most beautiful skyscraper. Like many of New York's buildings from the 1920s and 1930s, it is decorated with sculptures and metalwork in a style called art deco. Art deco uses geometric forms, smooth lines, and streamlined shapes. It was inspired by airplanes, fast ships, and cars.

The Empire State Building became the world's tallest building in 1931. It has 102 stories and measures 381 meters from the sidewalk to the roof. From the observation platform, you can see 125 kilometers on a clear day.

The building quickly became a symbol of New York. In the 1933 movie, *King Kong*, the giant gorilla climbs the skyscraper. King Kong thinks it is a safe place like the mountains on the island he comes from, but gets shot down by airplanes. In 1945, a real airplane crashed into the 79th floor of the building. But the Empire State Building is so strong there wasn't much serious damage. The crash happened at night when the building was empty, so few people were hurt. The building also has a 46 meter high mast. The idea was that giant passenger balloons called airships could dock there. Today, the mast is used as a radio and TV antenna.

The Empire State Building.

The Empire State Building is also decorated with art deco sculptures. Compared with the Chrysler Building, however, it is very simple. By 1931, America was in an economic crisis. Nearly one out of three people were out of work. There wasn't any money for fancy decoration. It was also hard to rent out all the office space. Many of the offices stayed empty until the 1940s. People called the building "the Empty State Building."

freaky facts:

The top 30 floors of the Empire State Building light up at night in different colors. Normally it is white. Red, white, and blue mark holidays like the 4th of July, which is America's birthday. Red is used for Valentine's Day and for Fire Department Memorial Day. Blue marks Police Memorial Day. Red and green are used during Christmas and Yellow and white for Easter. Colors also celebrate the city's many ethnic groups. There is green for the Irish on St. Patrick's Day; blue, white, and blue for Jewish holidays; red, black, and green for Dr. Martin Luther King Day; blue and white for Greek Independence Day; red, yellow, and green for Portugal Day; red and white for Polish Pulaski Day; black, yellow, and red for German Unification Day; green, white, and orange for India Independence Day; and green and white for Pakistan Independence Day. You can even see lavender and white for Gay Pride Day. There are also many other days with special lighting.

The lights are turned off during the spring and fall when birds migrate. The lights can confuse the birds.

The World Trade Center.

In 1972, New York got an even higher building. In fact, New York got two. The World Trade Center had two twin towers. Each tower was 110 stories and 411 meters tall. Each tower had 104 passenger elevators and 21,800 windows. One tower had an observation platform at the top. The other one had a restaurant called Windows on the World. The buildings had over a million square meters of offices, stores, and restaurants. 50,000 people worked in the World Trade Center, and up to 80,000 people visited it every day. A French acrobat, Philippe Petite, walked on a tightrope from one tower to the other in 1974. Another man invented special gloves and shoes and climbed up the outside of one of the towers like a human fly. Both men were arrested by the police. In 1977, King Kong climbed the Twin Towers in a remake of the old movie. But giant gorillas were not the only danger.

The World Trade Center was not the world's biggest building after 1974. Chicago has a building that is 442 meters tall. Even Taiwan got into the act. Right now, the 508-meter tall Taipei 101 in Taipei is the world's tallest skyscraper. Even so, the World Trade Center had become a symbol of New York. The towers also represented America's power and influence. On February 26th, 1993, Muslim terrorists exploded a bomb in the underground garage of one of the towers. 6 people were killed and more than 1,000 were injured.

But worse was to come. At 8.48 A.M. on September 11, 2001, an airliner crashed into the north tower and exploded in flames. At 9.03, another airplane flew into the south tower. Many people jumped to their deaths rather than get burned alive from the fire. At 10.05, the World Trade Center collapsed. New York had just experienced the biggest terrorist attack in history. 2,819 people were dead – including the airplane passengers. Six buildings were destroyed and about 100,000 jobs were lost.

Now New Yorkers must decide what will happen. Architect Daniel Libeskind plans to build a 541-meter tall tower. The tower will be called the 1776 building. In the US, most people don't use meters; they use feet. 541 meters equals 1776 feet. But 1776 also marks the year the US became an independent country. The tower will be the tallest skyscraper in the world, but part of the area will also be a museum and a memorial for the dead. The new tower is supposed to show the world that life goes on – even after great tragedies. It will serve as a symbol of America's strength and democracy.

Southern Manhattan during the collapse of the World Trade Center.

Bridges and Tunnels

A city with over 8 million people needs a lot of roads and highways. Since New York City consists of a series of islands, you also need a lot of bridges and tunnels to connect the different parts of the city.

New York's most famous bridge is the 1,825-meter long Brooklyn Bridge. The bridge opened in 1883 and was the first bridge over the East River. It took 14 years to build and was the biggest bridge in the world. Building the bridge cost the lives of many workers. Its first architect, John Augustus Roebling, was killed, so the bridge was finished by his son, Washington Roebling. Many of the workers got sick or died from a disease called "the bends." The bridge builders worked in airtight containers, called caissons, on the bottom of the East River. Air was pumped down to them under pressure. However, if the men got up too quickly from the caissons, tiny nitrogen bubbles in their bloodstream expanded and crippled them. Washington Roebling caught "the bends" in 1872 and became a cripple. For the next 11 years, he directed construction from an apartment in Brooklyn. He used field glasses to see what was going on and had his wife bring messages to the workers.

Brooklyn Bridge.

East River at night.

freaky facts:

New York's 7,600 sanitation workers (garbage collectors) remove 13,000 tons of garbage every day. The city has 2,000 garbage trucks. On Staten Island there are dumps where the garbage is piled as high as 75 meters.

Two tunnels and six more bridges cross the East River. One of New York's most beautiful sights is to see these bridges lit up at night.

Just one bridge, the 1,451-meter long George Washington Bridge, crosses the Hudson River and connects Manhattan and New Jersey. 50 million cars use it every year. But two car tunnels, five train tunnels, and ferries tie the city to New Jersey, too.

The Verrazano-Narrows Bridge.

Another record holding bridge is the Verrazano-Narrows Bridge linking Staten Island and Brooklyn. When it opened in 1964, this 4,176-meter suspension bridge was the longest in the world.

Some of the car tunnels are big. The Brooklyn-Battery Tunnel is 2,779 meters long. But New York's longest tunnels don't carry traffic; they carry water. At first, New Yorkers got their water from ponds and wells. By the 19th century, there wasn't enough fresh water. Unclean water led to cholera epidemics that killed thousands of people. Water is also needed for putting out fires and for flushing toilets. Without lots of water, you can't have a big city. Since 1842, aqueducts and tunnels have brought fresh water from mountains and hills far north of Manhattan. The Catskill Aqueduct, for example, is 193 kilometers long.

New York's aqueducts are starting to get old. This leads to problems when they leak. They are deep underground, between 90 and 700 meters, so it is hard to get to them. Some of the tunnels are nearly 6 meters in diameter, so they hold a lot of water. When they leak, it is a big leak. Experts say that the tunnels lose more than 1.6 billion liters of water every day! But they cannot simply shut off the aqueducts and take a look. The water pressure in the tunnels may be the only thing holding them up. So how do you find the leaks? Experts dropped a miniature, 2.6-meter long, remote-controlled submarine into the aqueducts. The submarine has cameras and computers to help find the leaks and take pictures. Later on, experts can analyze the pictures and try to come up with a solution.

Right now the city is building a new tunnel for water. This tunnel has a diameter of 7 meters and is being bored through the city's bedrock 140 to 245 meters below Manhattan's streets.

New York's most famous tunnels, however, are the tunnels of the subway system. New York's subway moves 1.3 billion passengers each year. The subway is so famous that it has been used in lots of movies. There are old stations and tracks that passengers have not seen for years. Some of them are used when movie makers want to shoot a subway scene. In the 1933 classic *King Kong*, the giant gorilla wrecks an elevated line. In 1986, *Crocodile Dundee* gets carried over the heads of the passengers in a crowded station to get to his girlfriend.

The subway system has over 1,300 kilometers of tracks, including train yards and storage areas. Around 112 kilometers of tracks run right above the city's streets. Once you pay your fare, you can stay on the subway as long as you like – it runs 24 hours a day. So if you want to, you can try out all 468 stations – it will probably take you a few days.

A subway station.

freaky facts:

Many people connect graffiti with New York's subways. In the 1970s, subway cars were completely covered with graffiti. Some people thought this graffiti was a new exciting kind of art. Most New Yorkers hated it. Graffiti made them feel unsafe. Nowadays, you won't see graffiti on subway cars. The city cracked down on graffiti artists and improved security in the train yards.

Schools

New York City has the biggest public school system in the United States. The city uses $12 billion each year on schools. There are more than a thousand schools. The city's schools have more than a million students.

New York has ordinary high schools like everywhere else in the USA. But New York also has many specialized schools. These schools are for talented students. Students have to take a special test to get into the specialized schools. If they are lucky, they can get into schools like the Bronx High School of Science; the Brooklyn Technical High School; the High School for Math, Engineering and Science; the High School of American Studies, and the High School of Music and Art and Performing Arts. At these and other schools, students can study everything from fashion design and ballet to cosmetology, journalism, and law.

Elementary school pupils in Brooklyn.

Dancers performing at the High School for Performing Arts.

Some of these schools are world famous. At the High School of Music and Art and the Performing Arts, students study painting, sculpture, graphics, music, singing, dancing, and acting. Many of the students dream about becoming stars one day on Broadway or in Hollywood. Celebrities like Liza Minnelli and Al Pacino went there. The musical, *Fame*, is about the hopes, ambitions, loves, and dreams of these teenagers. *Fame* was even turned into a TV series. Each year, the High School of Music and Art and the Performing Arts accepts about 800 new students. Up to 15,000 young people apply to get in!

The city's schools have lots of problems. Many well-to-do families send their children to private schools. They are afraid that the city's schools just aren't good enough. In fact, about 300,000 students go to private schools. This means that the public schools are left with lots of children from ethnic minorities or poor neighborhoods. A lot of these children do not speak English. About 134,000 of them are taught English in school. Only about 40% of the pupils in elementary schools meet reading standards. Even fewer of them meet math standards. However, the schools in poor neighborhoods do have special programs to help these children. Since teenage pregnancy is a big problem in poor neighborhoods, there are even special programs for pregnant girls. On the other hand, the specialized schools attract students from all over the city, no matter what race or background.

Capital of the World

freaky facts:

New York's taxis have been yellow since 1907. Yellow is the easiest color for the human eye to see.

Each year, about 17 million tourists come to New York from all over the world. Why?

New York is exciting and dramatic. There is nothing else in the world like the view of Manhattan from Brooklyn or the Staten Island ferry. The skyscrapers rise spectacularly above the water like some kind of magical fairy-tale castle. At night, the skyscrapers are like galaxies of stars. In the Wall Street area, the streets are like man-made canyons. Times Square glows at night with hundreds of giant neon ads. People come to Broadway's theaters to see dazzling musicals. New York's broad avenues pulse with people and taxis – in fact, there are more than 12,000 of them.

People also come to New York because of their jobs. New York's big banking and financial institutions have workers from all over. People from many different countries were killed when the World Trade Center was attacked on September 11, 2001.

Other foreigners work in New York because they are diplomats. New York is the capital of the world. Since 1947 the headquarters of the United Nations has been in New York. More than 180 countries belong to the UN. They meet in beautiful buildings along the East River. Actually, the UN is in New York, but it is not part of New York. It is not even part of the United States. The 7.3 hectares of the UN building and park are international territory. The UN even has its own postage stamps.

The UN Building.

Many New Yorkers hate the UN. Diplomats have something called diplomatic immunity. The city cannot do anything if a diplomat does something wrong. So many diplomats park their cars all over the place. They even park in front of fire hydrants. They just ignore the parking tickets. Diplomats owe New York $21.3 million. Egypt alone owes $1.9 million on more than 18,000 parking tickets! Some diplomats also run away from bills for food. They also forget to pay their rent.

On the other hand, the UN creates many jobs. About 16,000 people work at the UN Building. 30,000 people work for the many embassies and consulates that are in New York because of the UN. Thousands of people who work in restaurants and other service industries also owe their jobs to the UN. 420,000 people visit the UN each year. This creates jobs too.

Broadway.

Cultural Capital of the USA

A hundred years ago, many Americans felt that the US was inferior to Europe when it came to culture. Europe had everything America did not have. Europe had old paintings, old buildings, and great artists. On the other hand, the US had some of the richest people in the world. Many of these millionaires lived in New York. They wanted New York to be a great cultural city, too. They wanted the best that money could buy. They built opera houses and concert halls and paid famous conductors and singers to come to New York. New York also developed a theater tradition. Broadway became the place to go if you wanted to see plays or musicals.

freaky facts:

Many of the African animals at the American Museum of Natural History were shot by US President Theodore Roosevelt (president 1900 to 1908) who gave them to the museum.

These rich people liked to travel around Europe. If they saw furniture, paintings, sculptures or even a church or a castle they liked, they just bought it. Thanks to these people, New York has the best museums in the world. If you visit the Metropolitan Museum of Art, you can see a Roman room from Pompeii, a complete temple from ancient Egypt, and a whole three-story courtyard from a Renaissance palace, along with dozens of rooms from other European houses and palaces. The museum also has American art, world-famous paintings, suits of armor, musical instruments, and costumes.

New York has lots of other museums. The American Museum of Natural History has dinosaur skeletons, gems and minerals, stuffed birds and animals, shrunken heads, a planetarium, and thousands of other things. It is one of the biggest museums in the world.

freaky facts:

If you want to see the real Winnie-the-Pooh, you will have to go to New York's Public Library. Winnie-the-Pooh, the main character in a famous English children's book – and a series of Disney cartoons – was originally a teddy bear. He was bought at Harrods, a department store in London, for Christopher Robin, the author's son, who was another character in the stories. Some Englishmen think Pooh ought to be in England and not in the US. They even tried to get the English government to do something about it. In the end, the government decided that Winnie-the-Pooh was safe and happy in New York.

The Metropolitan Museum of Art.

Culture in New York is much more than just museums. In the 20th century, New York became the cultural center of the USA – maybe even of the world. For one thing, American artists became more confident. They found out that they did not need Europe for inspiration. In fact, many artists, musicians, filmmakers, and architects moved from Europe to America. In the 1930s and 1940s, many intellectuals had to flee from the Nazis. New York became their new home. But New York also became the center of exciting new kinds of American art and music.

In the 1930s and 40s, black jazz musicians like Count Basie, Louis Armstrong, and Duke Ellington played at clubs in Harlem. Jazz was important in the development of black pride. White audiences came to Harlem to hear black musicians. Soon black and white musicians were playing together in the same bands. Jazz is still important in New York. At the Village Vanguard, a club in Greenwich Village, you might even hear Woody Allen perform. Woody Allen is a famous filmmaker and comedian. Many of his movies take place in New York and make fun of New Yorkers, but jazz is Woody Allen's big hobby.

During the 60s and 70s, New York was home to Pop Art. Pop Artists used images from America's popular culture in their paintings and sculptures. Roy Lichtenstein's paintings look like pictures from giant comic books. Swedish-born Claes Oldenburg made giant sandwiches and hotdogs out of painted plaster and cloth. Andy Warhol used pictures of well-known people like Marilyn Monroe or images from advertisements. Warhol became famous for his paintings of Campbell Soup cans and Coca-Cola ads. Warhol mass-produced his pictures and called his art studio "the factory."

Much modern culture comes from New York's minorities. Rap music was invented in New York City in the 1970s by DJ Kool Herc, who originally came from Jamaica. Herc started playing records on two turntables and mixed beats from two songs. Soon rap spread to the rest of the USA and the world. Rap

Woody Allen playing with his New Orleans Jazz Band.

A graffiti memorial.

music is inspired by the tough world of black inner-city life. Many of the texts are about sex, violence, guns, and crimes. For many young people from ethnic minorities it is important to have respect, power, and friendship. In ghetto environments young people may feel that they are outcasts. They feel that they have been rejected by society. Through gangs, underground music, hip-hop culture, and break-dancing they get self-respect and an identity. In hip-hop culture, New York City is called "East Side," Los Angeles is the "West Side."

Graffiti is also part of this underground culture. In the 60s, 70s, and 80s, New York became famous for its graffiti. Young people in tough neighborhoods like the South Bronx could create "fame" for themselves through graffiti. Graffiti artists call themselves "writers." They call their art "writing." Many New Yorkers would call it something else – vandalism. At night, subway trains were "bombed" – covered with names or "tags" and giant pictures and letters called "pieces."

Subway cars today are built of paint-resistant stainless steel. The big graffiti paintings, "pieces," can be easily washed off. Graffiti "writers" have moved to walls and playgrounds. These days, much of their work is legal. The "writers" have permission from the property owners. A recent trend in Bronx graffiti is the creation of "tributes" or "memorials." They are giant "pieces" that honor people who have died from drugs, violence, or AIDS.

Some graffiti artists moved from the streets to art galleries. Jean-Michel Basquiat and Keith Haring started out tagging the subways, but have become accepted in the art world. Jean-Michel Basquiat was born in Brooklyn. His family originally came from Haiti and Puerto Rico and many of his paintings reflect this cultural background. Other Basquiat pictures have something to do with New York City and its history. Basquiat has even used the Dutch settlers as a theme. His pictures are now shown all over the US and Europe. Sadly, Basquiat died of a heroin overdose in 1988. He was just 28 years old.

Manhattan seen from Queens.

New York – Ups and Downs

New York City has always had its ups and downs. The 1960s and 1970s were a time of crisis in the city. There was a lot of trouble between blacks and whites. There were violent riots. Crime increased. Middle-class people left the city because they felt scared and because taxes and housing costs were high. The more middle-class people who left, the worse it got. The city could not collect enough tax money to pay all the policemen, firemen, school teachers, garbage collectors and other people who keep New York running. The city fired thousands of people and cut back on services. Garbage collectors went on strike. Garbage piled up in the streets. The subway workers went on strike. People couldn't get to work. Even the policemen went on strike. More and more middle-class people got fed up with the dirt and problems. They fled from the city. Finally, in 1975, New York City went bankrupt.

During the 1980s, the city's economic situation got better. In 1989, David Dinkins became the city's first black mayor. The city still had a big problem with poverty. Immigrants poured into the city, but there weren't many jobs for people without skills who cannot speak English. The cost of land in Manhattan was so great that many small industries moved out. Old warehouses and factory space were turned into luxury apartments, art galleries, and studios. But this meant that there were even fewer jobs for unskilled workers.

To help businesses, New York bought up land in the slum sections of Brooklyn, the Bronx, Queens, and Staten Island. The city then rented or sold this land to industries. The industries left Manhattan, but they stayed in the city. This helped keep jobs and tax money in New York.

But life in New York really picked up again after 1993 when Rudolph W. Giuliani became mayor. Giuliani cracked down on crime, prostitution, and graffiti. The streets were cleaned up.

New Yorkers felt very confident on September 11, 2001. New York was doing well. The USA was doing well. The economy was good. More and more blacks were joining the middle class. People were making lots of money. It was a beautiful, sunny day.

The attack on the World Trade Center has shaken New Yorkers' confidence. Thousands of people were dead. Was the city really a safe place to be? No one feels safe anymore. The attack has also cost up to a 100,000 jobs. The job of cleaning up will cost billions of dollars.

Perhaps Daniel Libeskind's plans for a new skyscraper will help restore confidence in the city. It will also create thousands of new jobs.

What will New York City be like in the 21st century? It's hard to tell. Just think how much the city has changed since the days of the first Dutch settlers! New York is always changing and will change again in the future. There will always be people who want to move to the city of New York and take a big bite out of "the Big Apple."

Daniel Libeskind's plan for new skyscrapers.

Vocabulary

p. 5

Hispanic	lateinamerikanischer Herkunft

Welcome to the Big Apple!

p. 6

subway	U-Bahn
slums	Slums
drug	Rauschgift
violence	Gewalt

p. 7

capital	Hauptstadt
state	Einzelstaat, einer von Amerikas 50 Bundesstaaten
United Nations	die Vereinten Nationen, UN
(to) be located in	gelegen sein in
head of state	Staatsoberhaupt
(to) affect	beeinflussen
belief	Glauben
fashion	Mode
department store	Kaufhaus

p. 8

poor	schlecht
(to) pay	bezahlen
illegal immigrant	illegaler Einwanderer
ballet company	Balletttruppe
library	Bibliothek
delicious	köstlich, delikat
horse racing	Pferderennen
reward	Preis
branch	Zweig
nickname	Spitzname

Geography

p. 9

state	Einzelstaat, einer von Amerikas 50 Bundesstaaten
(to) be located in	gelegen sein in
corner	Ecke
harbor	Hafen
(to) separate	trennen
development	Entwicklung
port city	Hafenstadt
immigrant	Einwanderer
(to) arrive	ankommen
(to) stay	bleiben

p. 10

biggest bargain	größtes Schnäppchen
ferry	Fähre
trip	Fahrt
spectacular	imponierend
view	Aussicht
the Statue of Liberty	die Freiheitsstatue
steam	Dampf
fare	Fahrpreis
pedestrian	Fußgänger
borough	Stadtbezirk
separate	getrennt
village	Dorf
mainland	Festland

p. 11

(to) surround	umgeben
department store	Kaufhaus
wide	breit
difference	Unterschied
population	Bevölkerung
Hispanic	lateinamerikanischer Herkunft
slums	Slums
mainly	hauptsächlich
suburb	Vorort
mile	Meile = 1.609 Meter

p. 12

(to) cover	sich erstrecken über
crowded	überfüllt
outwards	nach außen
(to) surround	umgeben
upwards	nach oben
apartment building	Wohnhaus
bedrock	Felsgestein
billion	Milliarde
(to) consist of	bestehen aus
schist	Schiefer
foundation	Fundament
humid	feucht

Nieuw Amsterdam

p. 13

site	Stätte
pottery	Töpferwaren
heap	Haufen
shell	Muschelschale
grave	Grab
tribe	Stamm
explorer	Forschungsreisender
harbor	Hafen
Dutch	holländisch
crew	Besatzung
narrow	schmal, eng

p. 14

Far East	der Ferne Osten
unfortunately	leider
short cut	Abkürzung
after a while	allmählich
(to) realize	einsehen
(to) lead to	führen nach/zu
beaver	Biber
skin	Fell
(to) claim	Anspruch erheben
(to) discover	entdecken
settler	Siedler
tip	Spitze
huge	riesig
body of water	Wassermasse

bay	Bucht
Pacific Ocean	der Pazifik
(to) starve	verhungern
(to) mutiny	meutern

p. 15

guilder	holl. Gulden
bargain	Schnäppchen
private property	Privateigentum
drawing	Zeichnung
brick	Backstein
stepped gable	Treppengiebel
(to) protect	beschützen
edge	Rande
(to) mark	markieren
spot	Stelle
expensive	teuer
religious freedom	Religionsfreiheit
monument	Denkmal
hunter	Jäger
wildlife	Tierwelt
Teddy bear	Teddybär

p. 16

disaster	Katastrophe
(to) decide	beschließen
warship	Kriegsschiff
(to) leave behind	hinterlassen
(to) elect	wählen
city government	Stadtverwaltung
descendant	Nachkomme
cookie	Plätzchen
place name	Ortsname
coat of arms	Wappen
barrel	Tonne, Sack
flour	Mehl
(to) reflect	widerspiegeln
the origin	Ursprung

English New York

p. 17

settler	Siedler
(to) turn ... into	verwandeln in
(to) remind	erinnern an
his Lordship	seine Lordschaft
(to) owe	schulden
jail	Gefängnis
merchant	Kaufmann
(to) hire	heuern
(to) capture	erobern, gefangen nehmen
Execution Dock	Stelle in London, wo Seeräuber hingerichtet wurden
treasure	Schatz
(to) bury	vergraben

p. 18

violence	Gewalt
(to) treat	behandeln
(to) put down	niederwerfen
afterwards	nachher
(to) execute	hinrichten
(to) accuse	anklagen
(to) succeed	gelingen

New York and the American Revolution

p. 19

(to) surround	umgeben
fence	Zaun
(to) owe	schulden
costs	Kosten
(to) tax	besteuern
(to) throw	werfen
cargo	Ladung
government	Regierung
(to) punish	bestrafen
the American Revolution	der amerikanische Unabhängigkeitskrieg
(to) choose	wählen
(to) declare	erklären
independence	Unabhängigkeit
(to) celebrate	feiern
(to) tear down	abreißen

p. 20

celebration	Feier
(to) chase	verjagen
navy	Flotte
(to) capture	erobern
protection	Schutz
(to) boom	einen Aufschwung erleben
tavern	Wirtshaus
civil war	Bürgerkrieg
battle	Schlacht

New York Grows

p. 21

(to) swear in	jmdn. vereidigen
city hall	Rathaus
capital	Hauptstadt
never	nie
(to) return	zurückkehren
stock exchange	Börse
(to) raise money	Geld aufbringen
shipping	Schifffahrt
independent	unabhängig

p. 22

steamship	Dampfschiff
cargo	Ladung, Fracht
(to) pour in	hineinströmen
grid	Gitter
(to) remove	entfernen
wood	Wald
(to) level	ebnen
amazing	verblüffend

Central Park

p. 23

apartment building	Mietshaus
(to) dig	ausheben

p. 24

state	Einzelstaat, einer von Amerikas 50 Bundesstaaten
busy	verkehrsreich
(to) surround	umgeben
backyard	Hintergarten
character	Figur
(to) relax	sich entspannen
spooky	unheimlich
in memory of	zum Andenken an

New Yorkers and their Neighborhoods

p. 25

Dutch	holländisch
immigrant	Einwanderer
opportunity	Möglichkeit
condition	Verhältnis
poverty	Armut

p. 26

port	Hafenstadt
(to) receive	empfangen
(to) be allowed to	dürfen
(to) descend	abstammen

the Statue of Liberty	Freiheitsstatue
harbor	Hafen
framework	Gerüst, Rahmen
(to) support	unterstützen

p. 27

dozen	Dutzend
dreadful	furchtbar
slums	Slums
terrible	schrecklich
gradually	allmählich
American society	die amerikanische Gesellschaft
proud	stolz
origin	Herkunft
(to) celebrate	feiern
groceries	Lebensmittel

p. 28

(to) thrive	gedeihen
old-fashioned	altmodisch
jeweler	Juwelier
literary movement	literarische Bewegung
author	Schriftsteller
resident	Bewohner
Supreme Court	oberstes Gericht
judge	Richter

p. 29

drug	Rauschgift
soul food	traditionelle Gerichte, die die Schwarzen in den Südstaaten essen
crowded	überfüllt
community	Gemeinschaft
Garment District	Bezirk mit Kleiderfabriken
(to) share	teilen
(to) hire	anstellen
waiter	Kellner
ethnical	ethnisch
artist	Künstler
expensive	teuer
warehouse	Lager

p. 30

Midtown	ein Teil von Manhattan
(to) consist of	bestehen aus
office building	Bürogebäude
giant	riesig
plaza	Platz
deserted	verlassen
in recent years	in den letzten Jahren

Rich and Poor

p. 31

stranger	Fremder
(to) be struck with	erstaunt sein über
there are but two	es gibt nur zwei
relatively	verhältnismäßig
expensive	teuer
grocery store	Lebensmittelgeschäft
rent	Miete
tax	Steuer
suburb	Vorort
(to) afford	sich leisten können

p. 32

wealthy	wohlhabend
mile	Meile = 1.609 Meter
castle	Burg
mansion	herrschaftliches Wohnhaus
(to) tear down	abreißen
(to) replace	ersetzen
(to) furnish	möblieren
valuable	wertvoll
studio	Einzimmerappartement
view	Aussicht
rooftop garden	Dachgarten, Dachterrasse
townhouse	Reihenhaus

p. 33

(to) browse	sich umsehen (unverbindlich)
antique	Antiquität
slums	Slums
skill	Fähigkeit
education	Ausbildung
(to) mean	bedeuten
unemployed	arbeitslos
dependent	abhängig
welfare payment	Sozialhilfe, Beihilfe
(to) receive	bekommen
food stamp	besonderer Wertschein für den Einkauf von Essen
cash	Bargeld
(to) connect	verbinden
drug	Rauschgift
(to) tempt	verleiten
gang violence	Gewalt in Banden

p. 34

map	Karte
track	Gleis
(to) continue	fortsetzen
northwards	nordwärts
(to) discover	entdecken
tale	Geschichte
child abuse	Kindesmisshandlung
(to) share	teilen
it doesn't matter	es ist egal/ gleichgültig
cockroach	Küchenschabe
disease	Krankheit
(to) get rid of	loswerden
pest	Schädling

p. 35

gentrification	das Verfahren, in dem Häuser in armen Vierteln von wohlhabenderen Käufern renoviert werden
borough	Stadtteil
average income	Durchschnittseinkommen
largely	überwiegend
tough	hart
condominium	Eigentumswohnung
co-op	Genossenschaftswohnung
(to) attract	anziehen
gay	homosexuell
compared to	verglichen mit
subway	U-Bahn
shelter	Unterkunft
mentally ill	geisteskrank
drug addict	Drogensüchtiger
tough break	Tief

New York's Finest

p. 36

even	sogar, selbst
violence	Gewalt
immigrant	Einwanderer

native	einheimisch
riot	Krawall
Civil War	der amerikanische Bürgerkrieg (1861-1864)
Confederate States	während des Bürgerkriegs versuchten die Südstaaten sich loszureißen und ihr eigenes Land zu bilden, das "The Confederate States of America" hieß
volunteer	Freiwilliger
government	Regierung
(to) draft	einziehen
wounded	verletzt

p. 37

watchman	Nachtwächter
police force	Polizei
(to) get rid of	abschaffen
(to) capture	erobern
mayor	Bürgermeister
(to) rob	berauben
battle	miteinander kämpfen
crime rate	Kriminalität-(squote)
Zero Tolerance Policy	Null-Toleranz Politik
(to) urinate	urinieren
(to) beg	betteln
(to) crack down	scharf vorgehen
minor	kleiner, unbedeutend
message	Botschaft
serious	ernsthaft
(to) put up with sth.	etwas tolerieren
(to) improve	verbessern
drug	Rauschgift
cash	Bargeld
(to) receive	empfangen
weapon	Waffe
the border	Grenze
(to) connect	verbinden
(to) commit	begehen
Port Authority	die Hafenbehörde von New York und New Jersey

prevention	Vorbeugung
rescue	Rettung
emergency	Notsituation

p. 38

(to) vanish	verschwinden
burglary	Einbruch
auto theft	Autodiebstahl
case	Fall
rape	Vergewaltigung
avoid	(ver)meiden
victim	Opfer
police officer	Polizist
tough	hart
in the line of duty	im Dienst
(to) regard	betrachten
entertainment	Unterhaltung

p. 39

secret agent	heimlicher Agent
several	mehrere
lumberyard	Holzlager
fortunately	glücklicherweise
(to) escape	entkommen

Skyscrapers

p. 40

floor	Stockwerk
(to) keep upright	sich aufrecht halten
brick	Backstein
(to) support	stützen
valuable	wertvoll
frame	Gerüst

p. 41

giant	riesig
(to) be scared	Angst haben, bekommen
progress	Fortschritt
flatiron	(altmodisches) Bügeleisen
triangular	dreieckig
(to) be competing	konkurrieren, wetteifern
former	ehemalig
flagpole	Fahnenstange
(to) attach	festmachen
border area	Grenzgebiet

p. 42

smooth	glatt
sidewalk	Bürgersteig

observation platform	Aussichtsplattform
(to) dock	anlegen

p. 43

(to) compare with	vergleichen mit
fancy	teuer
(to) rent out	vermieten
memorial day	Gedenktag
(to) migrate	ziehen
(to) confuse	verwirren

p. 44

twin towers	Zwillingstürme
tightrope	Seil
remake	neue Version z.B. von einem Film

p. 45

(to) get into the act	einsteigen
power	Macht
influence	Einfluss
airliner	Flugzeug
(to) experience	erleben
(to) decide	beschließen
independent	unabhängig
memorial	Denkmal

Bridges and Tunnels

p. 46

(to) consist of	bestehen aus
the bends	Taucherkrankheit
airtight	luftdicht
caisson	Senkkasten
pressure	Druck
nitrogen	Stickstoff
(to) expand	wachsen
(to) cripple	zum Krüppel machen
(to) direct	leiten
field glasses	Fernglas
message	Mitteilung

p. 47

garbage	Abfall
sanitation worker	Müllmann
(to) remove	entfernen
dump	Müllabladeplatz
(to) light up	hell beleuchten

p. 48

suspension bridge	Hängebrücke
pond	Teich
well	Brunnen
cholera	Cholera
(to) flush	spülen
(to) leak	lecken, leck sein
remote-controlled submarine	ferngelenktes U-Boot

p. 49

bedrock	Felsgestein
subway	U-Bahn
(to) wreck	zerstören
track	Gleis
train yard	Rangierbahnhof
fare	Fahrpreis
exciting	spannend
(to) crack down	scharf vorgehen

Schools

p. 50

public	öffentlich
billion	Milliarde
high school	Gymnasium
science	Naturwissenschaft
engineering	Ingenieurwesen
performing arts	Tanz, Theater, Ballet u.a.

p. 51

(to) apply	sich bewerben
well-to-do	wohlhabend
elementary school	Grundschule, 1. bis 6. Klasse
pregnancy	Schwangerschaft

Capital of the World

p. 52

capital	Hauptstadt
exciting	spannend
view	Aussicht
spectacular	imponierend
fairy-tale	Märchen
castle	Burg
canyon	Tal, Kluft
(to) glow	glühen
(to) dazzle	überwältigen
United Nations	die Vereinten Nationen, UN
actually	in Wirklichkeit
postage stamp	Briefmarke

p. 53

fire hydrant	Hydrant
(to) owe	schulden
bill	Rechnung
rent	Miete
embassy	Botschaft

Cultural Capital of the USA

p. 54

conductor	Dirigent

p. 55

furniture	Möbel
painting	Gemälde
castle	Burg
ancient Egypt	das altertümliche Ägypten
courtyard	Hof
dozen	Dutzend, viele
suit of armor	Rüstung
gem	Edelstein
(to) stuff	(aus)stopfen
shrunken head	Schrumpfkopf
Winnie-the-Pooh	Pu der Bär
teddy bear	Teddybär
author	Verfasser
government	Regierung

p. 56

confident	selbstbewusst
(to) flee	flüchten
exciting	spannend
pride	Stolz
audience	Zuschauer
image	Bild
comic book	Comic
cloth	Stoff
advertisement	Reklame
original	ursprünglich
turntable	Plattenspieler
beat	Takt

p. 57

tough	hart
violence	Gewalt
power	Macht
environment	Umwelt
outcast	Ausgestoßener
(to) reject	ablehnen
society	Gesellschaft
gang	Bande
fame	Ruhm
subway car	U-Bahn-Wagen
resistant	widerstands-
stainless steel	rostfreier Stahl
legal	gesetzmäßig
permission	Erlaubnis
property	Eigentum
recent	neu(er)
tribute	Ehrung
memorial	Mahnmal
(to) honor	ehren
(to) reflect	widerspiegeln
Dutch settler	holländischer Siedler

New York – Ups and Downs

p. 58

trouble	Schwierigkeit
violent	gewaltsam
riot	Krawall
(to) increase	zunehmen
(to) feel scared	Angst haben
tax	Steuer
(to) collect	(hier) einziehen
garbage collector	"Müllmann"
(to) cut back	einschränken
(to) pile up	sich häufen
subway	U-Bahn
(to) get fed up	etwas satt haben
(to) flee	flüchten
bankrupt	bankrott
immigrant	Einwanderer
(to) pour into	einströmen
skill	Fähigkeit
warehouse	Lagerhaus
apartment	Wohnung
unskilled worker	ungelernter Arbeiter

p. 59

business	Geschäft
(to) rent	vermieten
(to) pick up	besser werden
(to) crack down on	scharf vorgehen gegen
confident	selbstsicher
billion	Milliarde
(to) restore	wiederherstellen
confidence	Selbstvertrauen
(to) create	schaffen
Dutch settler	holländischer Siedler